Cherokee Rose

Leni Donlan

Raintree

Chicago, Illinois

Designed by Kimberly R. Miracle and Betsy Wernert
Photo Research by Tracy Cummins
Maps on pages 13 and 24 by Mapping Specialists
Printed in China by Leo Paper Group

12 11 10 09 08
10 9 8 7 6 5 4 3 2 1

Library of Congress Cataloging-in-Publication Data
Donlan, Leni.
 Cherokee Rose : the Trail of Tears / Leni Donlan.
    p. cm. -- (American history through primary sources)
 Includes bibliographical references and index.
 ISBN 978-1-4109-2702-6 (hc) -- ISBN 978-1-4109-2713-2 (pb)
 1. Trail of Tears, 1838--Juvenile literature. 2. Cherokee Indians--History--Juvenile literature. 3. Cherokee Indians--Relocation--Juvenile literature. I. Title.
 E99.C5D67 2008
 973.04'97557--dc22
                          2007005963

Acknowledgments
The author and publisher are grateful to the following for permission to reproduce copyright material: Library of Congress Geography and Map Division **pp. 4, 8–9, 19**; Library of Congress Rare Book and Special Collections **pp. 5, 12 (right)**; Frank H. McClung Museum, The University of Tennessee. Artist Carlyle Urello **p. 6–7**; Library of Congress Prints and Photographs Division **pp. 9, 12 (left), 14, 17, 18**; The Granger Collection **pp. 11, 22–23, 28**; Western History/Genealogy Dept., Denver Public Library **pp. 15, 16, 29**; Newberry Library / SuperStock **p. 20**; James Robinson/ Animals Animals **p. 27**.

Cover image of THE TRAIL OF TEARS, 1838 (oil on canvas by Robert Lindneux), reproduced with permission of The Granger Collection.

The publishers would like to thank Isabel Tovar and Nancy Harris for their assistance in the preparation of this book.

Every effort has been made to contact copyright holders of any material reproduced in this book. Any omissions will be rectified in subsequent printings if notice is given to the publishers.

Contents

The Cherokee

The Cherokee are Native Americans. They have lived in North America for thousands of years. The Cherokee homeland was where seven states are now (see the map on page 13).

This map was made in the 1700s. Can you find the Cherokee land? (Hint: *Cherokee* is not spelled the way it is today.)

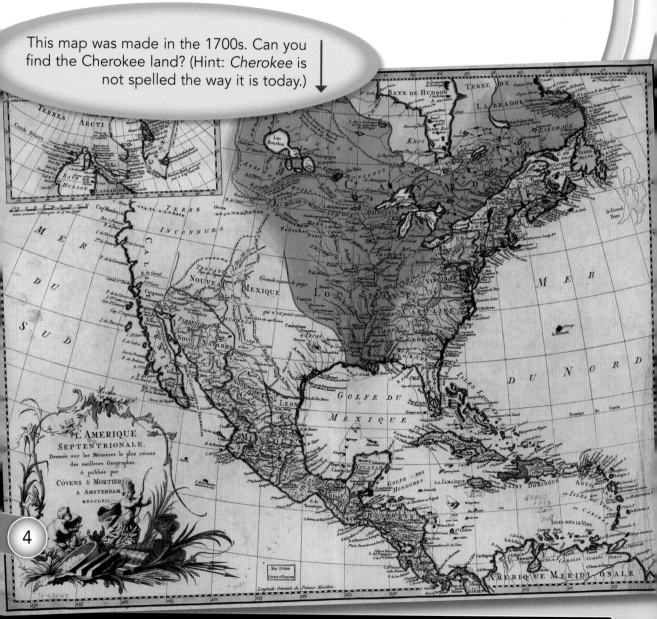

blowgun narrow pipe through which darts can be blown

Their land had mountains and valleys. It had rivers, lakes, and forests. Their land got a lot of rain. It had good soil. The Cherokee were able to grow many crops.

The Cherokee were hunters, too. They hunted with bows and arrows. They also hunted with **blowguns**. Blowguns are narrow pipes. Darts are blown through these pipes. They fished using spears and fishing poles. They traveled in **dugout canoes** (see box below).

The Cherokee people made **pottery**. Pottery is dishes and bowls made out of clay. They made baskets and clothing. They were able to make, hunt, or grow everything they needed to live.

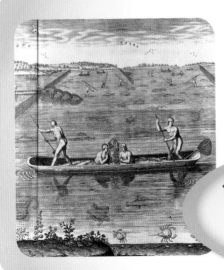

A dugout canoe is a boat made from a tree trunk. The inside of the tree is removed. This makes a place to sit. The ends of the canoe are shaped into points.

These Native Americans are fishing from a dugout canoe.

Cherokee life

The Cherokee lived in **villages**. A village is a community that is smaller than a town. Each village had a large, round building. It was called a town house. Around the town house was a **plaza** (open space). The town house and plaza were used for visits and meetings.

Cherokee family homes were outside the plaza. In the summer, families lived in large wooden houses. Their winter homes were smaller. They were built of woven sticks. Then they were covered with mud. A fire burned in the center of the winter home.

Each Cherokee village had a town **council**. A council was a group of people. They made decisions for the village.

The Cherokee believed that all things were important. The land, rivers, and oceans were important. Plants, animals, and people were all important. They believed that all living things needed one another.

The Cherokee believed in a great spirit. They felt this spirit created all life. These beliefs were passed from the older people to the younger ones.

council   group of people who make plans and decisions for everyone
plaza   open space around or between buildings
village   community of people that is smaller than a town

This is an example of a Cherokee village.

Two Worlds Meet

The Cherokee way of life began to change in the 1500s. That is when **European settlers** first arrived in Cherokee land. These people came from the continent of Europe. They planned to live in North America. Two worlds—Native American and European—met.

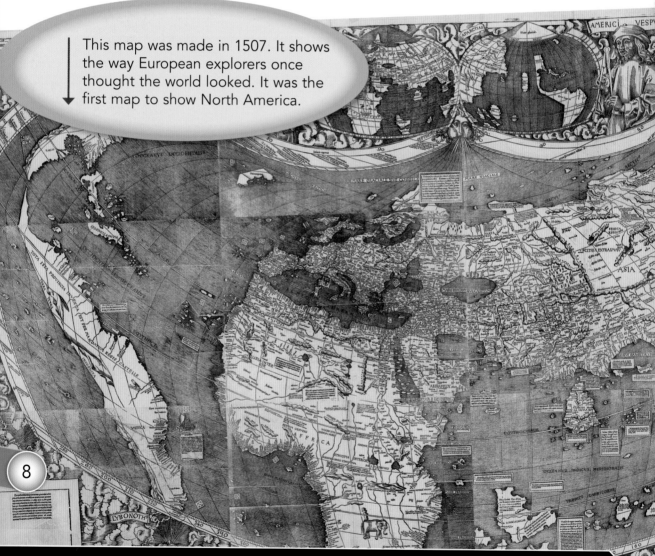

This map was made in 1507. It shows the way European explorers once thought the world looked. It was the first map to show North America.

European	person who comes from the continent of Europe
explorer	someone who finds or looks at new lands
settler	someone who goes to live in a place about which little is known

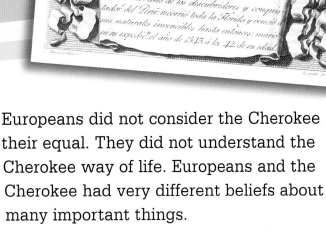

Hernando De Soto was an **explorer** from the country of Spain. Explorers find or look at new lands. He and his men were the first Europeans the Cherokee met.

Europeans did not consider the Cherokee their equal. They did not understand the Cherokee way of life. Europeans and the Cherokee had very different beliefs about many important things.

Europeans believed it was important to own land. Europeans used force to get the land they wanted. They fought wars to win more land from others.

The Cherokee believed that land could not be owned. They believed it could only be shared. The Cherokee did not believe in using force to take land.

9

Different beliefs

Europeans sometimes tried to control nature. They built dams to change the path of streams and rivers. They cut down trees to make land for large farms. They built fences around their land.

The Cherokee believed they must live in **harmony** with nature. They tried to get along with nature. They tried not to change nature too much.

Europeans did not understand what the Cherokee believed about owning land. But Europeans did know one thing. They knew that the Cherokee did not feel they owned their land. This made it easy for Europeans to take the Cherokee land.

Europeans lived in North America for many years. Over time, they began to think of North America as their home. They did not think the land belonged to Native Americans. They felt the land was theirs.

Chief Cumnacatogue traveled to London, England, in 1762. The chief (leader) met the king of England. Do you think this meeting helped Europeans understand the Cherokee?

harmony   agreement, getting along with

A New Country: The United States of America

The **Europeans** were **colonists**. Colonists are people who live in one country but are ruled by another country. The king of England ruled the colonists in North America. The colonists wanted to rule themselves. They fought a war against England.

President George Washington (below) sent this letter to the Cherokee people in 1796. The letter explains how the Cherokee can learn to fit in by acting like white people.

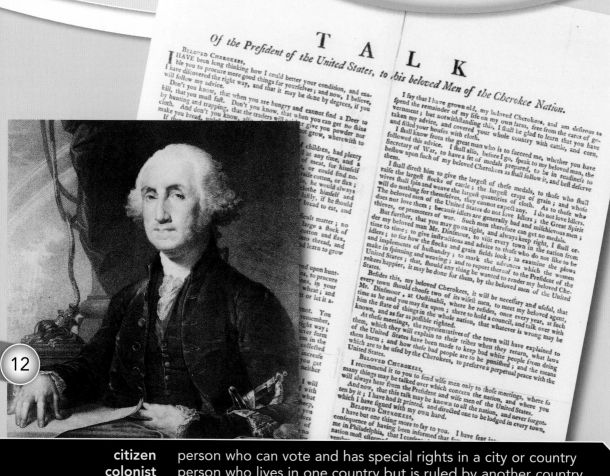

citizen	person who can vote and has special rights in a city or country
colonist	person who lives in one country but is ruled by another country

This map shows the United States in 1803. The red part shows the Cherokee land. It had been Cherokee land long before the U.S. was a country.

BRITISH CANADA

L. Superior

L. Michigan

L. Huron

L. Ontario

L. Erie

Vermont (1791)

Maine

New Hampshire

New York

Massachusetts

Rhode Island

Connecticut

Pennsylvania

New Jersey

Delaware

Ohio (1803)

Indiana Territory

Virginia

Maryland

Kentucky (1792)

Tennessee (1796)

North Carolina

South Carolina

Mississippi Territory

Georgia

SPANISH LOUISIANA

SPANISH FLORIDA

Gulf of Mexico

ATLANTIC OCEAN

N W E S

Cherokee Territory, 1791

0   150   300 miles
0   150   300 kilometers

The war was called the Revolutionary War. In 1783 the colonists won the war. The United States of America became a new country. The colonists became **citizens** of the United States. Citizens are people who vote for their leaders. Citizens are protected by the country's laws (rules).

Native Americans were not thought of as citizens. They had been in North America long before white people. But they were not protected by the laws of the United States.

George Washington was the first president of the United States. He led the country. He wanted Native Americans to live just like the citizens of the new country.

13

Changing the Cherokee

George Washington wanted the Cherokee to act like white people. So did the U.S. government.

The U.S. government sent white people to live with the Cherokee. They taught them how to live like they did. They taught Cherokee men how to use **plows** for farming. Plows are tools that break up the soil. Cherokee women were taught how to make cloth. They were given **spinning wheels** and **looms**. Spinning wheels turned cotton or wool into thread or yarn. Looms turned thread or yarn into cloth.

President Washington wanted the Cherokee to learn to use a spinning wheel.

boarding	giving meals and a place to sleep
loom	tool for turning thread or yarn into cloth
plow	farm tool used to break up the soil
spinning wheel	tool for turning cotton or wool into thread or yarn

Cherokee children were sent away from their families. They were sent to **boarding** schools. The children lived at the schools. They were taught to act like white children. They were taught to read, write, and do math, too.

The Cherokee wanted to live in peace with American **citizens**. Many Cherokee changed their way of living. Not all Cherokee were willing to give up living the old way, though. By 1800 some Cherokee began moving away from their homeland. They moved west. They moved to land that was far away from white people.

This boarding school was for Cherokee girls. They learned to act and dress like white women.

15

phabet and a newspaper

okee knew that being able to read and write was
t. A Cherokee named Sequoyah created a Cherokee
alphabet. This alphabet was used to read and write the
Cherokee language. It was very easy to use. The Cherokee
could learn to read and write in as little as two days!

A Cherokee named Elias Boudinot started the *Cherokee
Phoenix*. It was the Cherokees' first newspaper. It was
written in English and Cherokee. The *Cherokee Phoenix* was
like the newspapers the white people read. Many Cherokee
read the *Cherokee Phoenix*. Many white people in North
America and Europe read the *Cherokee Phoenix*, too.

This shows the
Cherokee alphabet.

FACSIMILE OF CHEROKEE ALPHABET BEFORE PRINTING.

1 A, short. 2 A broad. 3 Lah. 4 Tsee. 5 Nah. 6 Weeh. 7 Weh. 8 Leeh. 9 Neh. 10 Mooh. 11 Keeh
12 Yeeh. 13 Seeh. 14 Clanh. 15 Ah. 16 Luh. 17 Leh. 18 Hah. 19 Woh. 20 Cloh. 21 Tah. 22 Yahn.
23 Lahn. 24 Hee. 25 Ss (sibilant.) 26 Yoh. Un (French.) 28 Hoo. 29 Goh. 30 Tsoo. 31 Maugh. 32 Seh.
33 Saugh. 34 Cleegh. 35 Queegh. 36 Quegh. 37 Sah. 38 Quah. 39 Gnaugh (nasal.) 40 Kaah. 41 Tsahn
42 Sahn. 43 Neeh. 44 Kah. 45 Taugh. 46 Keh. 47 Taah. 48 Khan. 49 Weeh. 50 Eeh. 51 Ooh. 52 Yeh.
53 Un. 54 Tun. 55 Kooh. 56 Tsoh. 57 Quoh. 58 Noo. 59 Na. 60 Loh. 61. Yu. 62 Tseh. 63 Tee. 64
Wahn. 65 Tooh. 66 Teh. 67 Tsah. 68 Un. 69 Neh. 70 ——— 71 Tsooh. 72 Mah. 73 Clooh. 74 Haah. 75
Hah. 76 Meeh. 77 Clah. 78 Yah. 79 Wah. 80 Teeh. 81 Clegh. 82 Naa. 83 Quh. 84 Clah. 85 Maah 86
Quhn.

16

Sequoyah understood that the Cherokee needed to read and write. He created an alphabet.

Many Cherokee were able to change and live like white people. John and Lewis Ross became rich and succesful. They were the sons of a Cherokee mother and a white father. The Ross brothers owned homes and businesses. They were leaders in their community.

Tricked!: The Treaty of Echota

Andrew Jackson became president (leader) of the United States in 1829. He promised to treat Native Americans fairly. This was a lie.

In 1830 Jackson passed the **Indian Removal Act**. This law said that all Native Americans would be moved to Indian **Territory**. Indian Territory was an area of land west of the Mississippi River (see the map on page 19).

John Ross was chief of the Cherokee. The Cherokee trusted him. Ross tried to work with the U.S. government. He wanted to save the homeland of his people.

President Andrew Jackson was not a friend to Native Americans.

Indian Removal Act   law signed by President Andrew Jackson in 1830. It called for the movement of American Indians to lands west of the Mississippi River.

But the U.S. government wanted the Cherokee land. So, they tricked Ross and the Cherokee people. Instead of talking to Ross, they went to some other Cherokee men. These men were not the chosen leaders of the Cherokee. They were not allowed to make decisions for all of the Cherokee. The U.S. government did not care.

The U.S. government promised money and land to the these men. They would also get the best land in Indian Territory. These men signed an agreement with the U.S. government.

This map shows where Jackson wanted to send the Cherokee and other Native Americans.

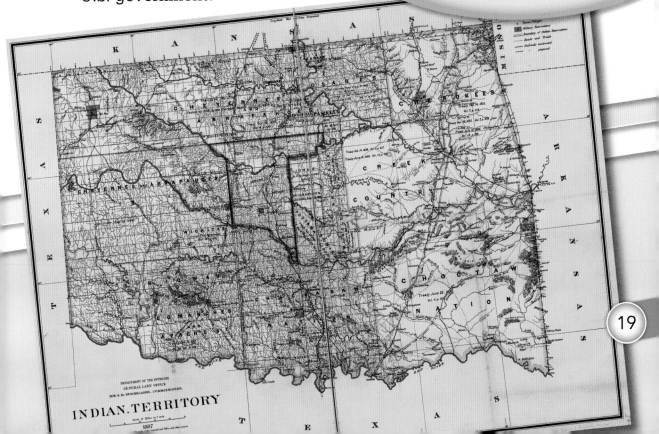

19

overturn change a decision involving a law

Treaty of New Echota agreement signed in New Echota, Georgia, that

Treaty of New Echota

Some of the Cherokee men signed the agreement. This happened in New Echota, Georgia, on December 29, 1835. The agreement is known as the **Treaty of New Echota**. In this agreement, all of the Cherokee land was sold to the U.S. government.

John Ross and other leaders did not agree with the Treaty of New Echota. They tried to stop it from becoming a law. But in May 1836 the Treaty of New Echota was made a law. The Cherokee land belonged to the U.S. government.

Some Cherokee had no hope left. They did not trust the government. They moved to Indian **Territory** on their own.

Ross and most of the Cherokee made no plans to move. They still thought they could save their land. They believed they could **overturn** (change) the new law. They were wrong. They could not change the decision. The Cherokee had to move out of what was the United States at this time. (See the map on page 24.)

John Ross was chief of the Cherokee nation from 1828 to 1866.

Removal:
The Trail of Tears

In May 1838, U.S. soldiers came to Cherokee lands. They rounded up the Cherokee people. The soldiers burned Cherokee homes. They burned their crops, too. Many Cherokee parents and children were **separated**. They were forced to go in different directions. Many Cherokee were hurt. Some were killed.

Private John G. Burnett, a member of the U.S. Army, saw the roundup. He led Cherokee to Indian **Territory**. Burnett said: "I saw the helpless Cherokees arrested and dragged from their homes.... I saw them loaded like cattle or sheep into 645 wagons and started toward the West.... The sufferings of the Cherokees were awful. The trail ... was a trail of death.... And I have known as many as 22 of them to die in one night."

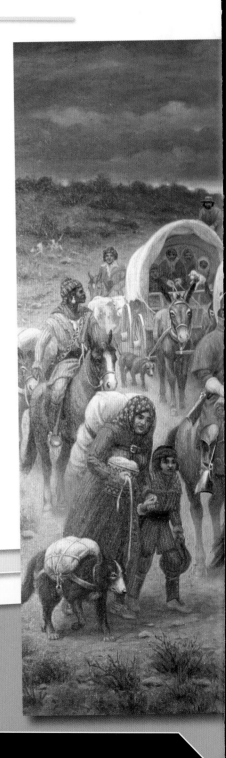

Hiding

Some Cherokee escaped the removal. They hid in the mountains. The soldiers did not find them.

22

separate   put in different directions

Cherokee travel in the freezing winter of 1838. The long journey is known as the "Trail of Tears."

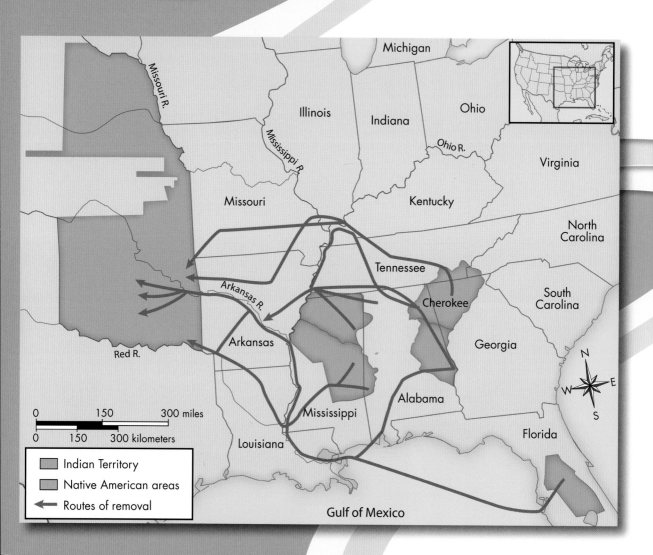

This map shows how the Cherokee and other Native American groups moved to Indian Territory.

Michigan

Missouri R.

Illinois

Indiana

Ohio

Ohio R.

Virginia

Mississippi R.

Missouri

Kentucky

North Carolina

Tennessee

Arkansas R.

Cherokee

South Carolina

Arkansas

Georgia

Red R.

Alabama

0   150   300 miles
0   150   300 kilometers

Mississippi

Florida

Louisiana

Indian Territory

Native American areas

Routes of removal

Gulf of Mexico

drought   long period of dry weather

A terrible journey

Some Cherokee were moved to Indian **Territory** by water. Three groups traveled by river. There were almost 2,800 people in these groups. The first group left on June 6, 1838. The Cherokee who traveled by river suffered. There was **drought** (dry weather) and illness. They did not arrive in Indian Territory until the end of the summer.

The rest of the Cherokee traveled to Indian Territory over land. They were in groups of 700 to 1,600 people. Each group had a leader and an assistant leader. John Ross chose the leaders.

The Cherokee traveled with food, but there was not enough. Drought made it hard for the animals. Most people walked almost 1,000 miles (1,600 kilometers).

Bad roads and winter storms made the trip even harder. There was also illness. People died every day.

In 1838 and 1839, 11,500 Cherokee were moved from their homeland. They were moved to a new home in Indian Territory (see the map). Almost 4,000 Cherokee died along the way.

A survivor's story

Lilian Anderson is the granddaughter of Washington Lee. Washington Lee was a child in 1838. He and his family walked on the Trail of Tears. This is what Lee told Lilian.

Somewhere along the trail, Lee lost his family. He never saw his mother, father, or sister again.

There were government wagons. The wagons carried supplies. But they did not bring enough food or water. The food they did bring was bad. Sometimes there was no water for two or three days. Some old people were too weak to walk. They rode in the wagons. Everyone else walked.

Lee's aunt, Chin, walked on the trail with her family. First, her husband died. Aunt Chin was left with three small children. She took one child by the hand. She carried the two other children. All three children died on the trail. Aunt Chin buried them by the side of the Trail of Tears.

The Cherokee Rose

It is said that the mothers of the Cherokee cried and cried. The chiefs wanted to stop the women's crying. They wanted the women to be strong so they could care for their children. The chiefs prayed for a sign. From that day on, a beautiful rose grew wherever a mother's tear touched the ground. The Cherokee Rose still grows along the **route** (path) of the "Trail of Tears."

Today, the Cherokee Rose is the state flower of Georgia.

route   road or path followed

The Cherokee Today

In the Indian **Territory**, the Cherokee got adjusted to their new homeland. They created a system of government to lead the homeland. They created a school system. Sadly, the Cherokee lost land again and again. This happened over the next 100 years.

The Cherokee have tried to hold on to their beliefs and **traditions**. These include thoughts and practices passed down over time. Like other American **citizens**, they work and go to school. They take care of their families.

This is a copy of the *Cherokee Phoenix* from 1828. The *Phoenix* is still published today!

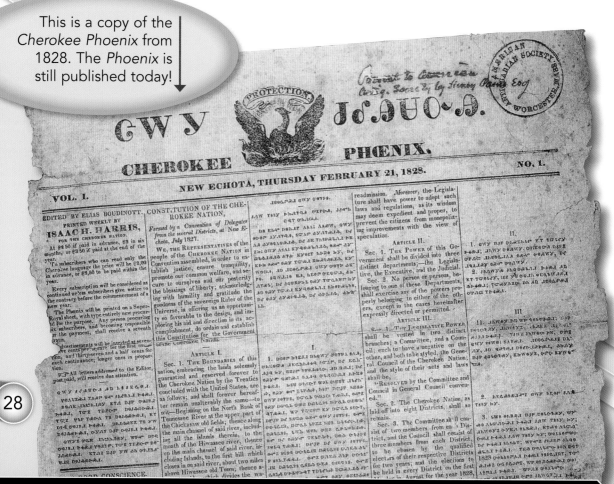

descendant — person related to you who lives after you
historian — person who studies history
tradition — thoughts and practices passed down over time

Today, most **descendants** (relatives) of the Cherokee are still in the West. Cherokee are back in North Carolina, too. They are called the Eastern Band of Cherokee. They are the descendants of the earlier Cherokee. Some of their relatives hid in the hills during the removal. Some made their way back east after removal.

Native Americans have suffered at the hands of white people. The Cherokee story is very sad. The Cherokee tried everything they could to fit in. But white people never accepted them as just men, women, and children. Richard White is a **historian**. He studies history. Richard White said: "In the end, being Indian is what kills them."

The Cherokee remember the Trail of Tears.

THE SITE OF
OLD CHEROKEE TRAIL

THIS MONUMENT IS
ERECTED BY
MRS. R. D. MEYER
HANNA, WYOMING
JUNE 1914

Glossary

blowgun narrow pipe through which darts can be blown

boarding giving meals and a place to sleep

citizen person who can vote and has special rights in a city or country

colonist person who lives in one country but is ruled by another country

council form of government in which a group of people plans and makes decisions for everyone

descendant person related to you who lives after you

drought long period of dry weather

dugout canoe boat with pointed ends that is made from a tree trunk

European person who comes from the continent of Europe

explorer person who looks for new land

harmony agreement, getting along with

historian person who studies history

Indian Removal Act law signed by President Andrew Jackson in 1830. It called for the movement of American Indians to lands west of the Mississippi River.

loom tool for turning thread or yarn into cloth

overturn change a decision involving a law

plaza open space around or between buildings

plow farm tool used to break up the soil

pottery clay dishes and bowls

route road or path to be followed

separate put in different directions

settler someone who goes to live in a place about which little is known

spinning wheel tool for turning cotton or wool into thread or yarn

territory area of land

tradition thoughts and practices passed down over time

Treaty of New Echota agreement signed in New Echota, Georgia, that forced the Cherokee to move from their homeland

village community of people that is smaller than a town

Want to Know More?

Books to read

- Bruchac, Joseph. *The Journal of Jesse Smoke: A Cherokee Boy, Trail of Tears, 1838*. New York: Scholastic, 2001.

- Rumford, James. *Sequoyah: The Cherokee Man Who Gave His People Writing*. Boston: Houghton Mifflin, 2001.

- Underwood, Thomas Bryan. *Cherokee Legends and the Trail of Tears*. Minneapolis, MN: Sagebrush, 1998.

Websites

- http://cherokee.org/home.aspx?section=culture&culture=kids
  The official site of the Cherokee Nation.

- http://www.americaslibrary.gov/cgi-bin/page.cgi/jb/nation/tears_1
  Learn more about John Ross and the Trail of tears.

Read **Counting Coup: Customs of the Crow Nation** to find out about the history and traditions of the Crow people.

Read **The Birth of a State: California Missions** to find out who built these lovely missions and why.

Index